Don't Agonize, Organize Your Office Now!

This publication is designed to provide accurate and authoritative information in regard to the subject matter covered. The information in this book is true and complete to the best of our knowledge. It is sold with the understanding that the author and publisher are not engaged in rendering legal, accounting or other professional services. All recommendations are made without guarantee on the part of the author or publisher. The author and publisher disclaim any liability or responsibility to any person or entity with respect to any loss or damage caused, or alleged to be caused, directly or indirectly by the information contained in this book. Although every precaution has been taken in the preparation of this book, the author and publisher assume no responsibility for errors or omissions. No warranty or fitness is implied.

All rights reserved. No part of this book may be used or reproduced in any manner whatsoever without written permission of the author except in the case of brief quotations in a review with appropriate credits; nor may any part of this book be stored in a retrieval system or transmitted in any form by any means-electronic, mechanical, photocopying, recording or other-without written permission from the author.

Copyright © 2008 Diane A. Hatcher
All rights reserved.
ISBN: 1-4196-5866-2
ISBN-13: 978-1419658662
Library of Congress Control Number: 2007900822

BookSurge, LLC
North Charleston, South Carolina

DIANE A. HATCHER-CPO®

DON'T AGONIZE, ORGANIZE YOUR OFFICE NOW!

SIMPLE SOLUTIONS FOR YOUR OFFICE ORGANIZING CHALLENGES

Don't Agonize, Organize Your Office Now!

TABLE OF CONTENTS

DEDICATION ix
INTRODUCTION xi

1. FEELING THE NEED TO ORGANIZE 1
2. FACING OUR FEARS 3
3. AFFLUENZA AND DISPOSAPHOBIA 7
4. ARE YOU CHRONICALLY DISORGANIZED? 11
5. PROCRASTINATION IN THE OFFICE 15
6. IT'S NOT ABOUT PERFECTION 19
7. THE COST OF CORPORATE CLUTTER 23
8. RIDING THE RAFT TO SUCCESS 27
9. SIX EASY STEPS TO REDUCING PAPER. 33
10. FILING 101 FOR SMARTIES 37
11. ORGANIZING THOSE PESKY RECEIPTS. . . . 43
12. FUN WITH OFFICE SUPPLIES 47
13. ORGANIZING THE OFFICE SUPPLY
    CABINET 51
14. PRACTICAL TIPS FOR SAVING TIME
    AT WORK 55
15. THE SECRET TO TIME MANAGEMENT 59
16. TEN SMART PACKING TIPS 63
17. YOUR LIFETIME TRAVEL LIST 67
18. WHY HIRE A PROFESSIONAL
    ORGANIZER? 71
19. SCHEDULING A DAY IN 77
20. ODE TO AN ORGANIZER 81

*To my husband Don, who is my rock and my best friend,
for all his support for everything I do.
To my daughters, Heather and Haley, of whom I am
most proud.
To all my fellow professional organizers, whom I admire
and respect for their support and dedication to this
wonderful profession.
To everyone who helped me bring this book to fruition, your
time and intelligence is greatly appreciated.
And to my clients, the nicest people in the world who have
trusted me enough to invite me into their homes and offices,
inspired me, and given me the motivation to continue
helping others.*

INTRODUCTION

The only major pitfall or drawback to being a professional organizer is that some people equate that with being perfect.

Being organized is not about being perfect. We are all still human and prone to errors. I like to tell people that the difference between an organized person and one who is not, is that when an organized person makes a mistake (like misplacing one's keys), he/she devises a solution so that the same mistake is not repeated.

Ironically, sometimes perfection stops people from trying to be organized. When life circumstances get in their way, they are prone to stop being as meticulous or detail-oriented as they once were. This could be due to time constraints, depression, physical disability and the like. Their surroundings then spiral out of control and they feel hopeless and overwhelmed about ever getting back to being organized.

Whether that has happened to you or someone you know the answers lie in this little book.

Attorneys, doctors, professionals of all kinds, and people who work from home and in the home, will all find what they need in the pages of this book.

I am often approached about whether I have experience working in law offices, accounting offices, etc. Although I have organized offices in most every field, that is not the important factor here. What I need to know is how to help you deal with paperwork, filing systems, mail, email, phone calls and time management. Anyone who works in an office or runs a business deals with these issues and that is what you all have in common. This is where my expertise lies. With the systems that I have devised and share in *Don't Agonize, Organize Your Office Now*, you too will benefit.

So enjoy your journey as you navigate the waters of this book. You can look forward to getting yourself organized.

I invite you to visit my website at www.timesaversusa.com and sign up for my free monthly e-zine to help support you along your organizing journey.

Happy Organizing!

CHAPTER 1
FEELING THE NEED TO ORGANIZE

How do you feel when you walk into your office each morning?

If you love being in your office every day, this book probably isn't for you. But if, shortly after arriving at work, you feel grouchy, stressed, tired, distracted, unfocused, or tense, this book can help you.

Think about your jaw, shoulders, neck, and stomach. Do these areas tense up when you arrive at work? If so, you may be experiencing an emotional response to your environment. Dr. Cindy Spellman, a psychiatrist and former Ft. Lauderdale, Florida, resident, recognized these feelings within herself. "I read a book about organizing and realized where the resistance to working at my desk was coming from. Inside I was reacting to the mess surrounding me and didn't realize it."

Studies have shown that when we walk into our office and see clutter and papers piled everywhere, an emotional response occurs—whether or not we are aware of it. Typically, we feel drained, de-energized. Dr. Spellman (who was also my client) explains that outer chaos and disorder make people feel more vulnerable and less in control of their lives. "The more disordered the world {as it has been since September 11, 2001} the more the need for order in our surroundings."

What's the solution to our work-space-induced stress? Get organized. Because we can't throw out all the papers on our

1

desk and floor without sorting and making decisions on them, however, we'll need to follow a process. In other words, we need to be organized about getting organized.

This book will take you through all the steps you need to create an organized work environment. We will look at some of the obstacles to becoming organized, how organizing improves a business' bottom line, and how to build a RAFT for navigating the river of paper that floods our lives. So climb aboard and enjoy the ride. After all, as Dr. Spellman can testify, "The feelings of freedom and control of my surroundings that I feel since organizing my office came immediately and have lasted. It feels so good. I really enjoy sitting at my desk and working now."

CHAPTER 2
FACING OUR FEARS

Have you tried repeatedly to organize your office, your papers, your clutter, or your life—but with each attempt, some negative feeling stopped you? Then, in order to avoid that feeling, you quit, gave up? That feeling you felt was fear.

Acknowledging our need to get organized can trigger a wide array of uncomfortable reactions. It can force us to face our fear of change, our fear of failure, our fear of humiliation, of embarrassment, shame, frustration, or criticism. It can shine a bright spotlight on our difficulties with focus and making decisions. It can bring up feelings of overwhelm, make us admit that we're perfectionists.

Organizing can also set off internal conflicts. For example, sometimes a well-intentioned relative or friend tells us that we "should" be able to get organized on our own. This sets off the inner-parent voice in our head, the castigating voice that thrives on criticism and shame. Some of us rebel against this voice, adding an internal parent-child power struggle to our feelings of shame.

Another inner conflict arises when what's familiar to us no longer works. We often recreate our childhood surroundings. If our home while growing up was cluttered, then clutter can feel comfortably familiar. Eventually, though, clutter and disorganization create more problems than the comfort they provide, which gives rise to internal struggle. Venturing into unknown territory—even if it's an uncluttered room—can feel intimidating.

Remaining disorganized has its payoffs. Avoidance and denial can be (temporary) safe harbors. Familiarity breeds contempt? No, it provides illusions of safety. And nothing ventured, nothing gained? Just the opposite! "After all," think some, "what if I try to get organized, but fail? Then all my efforts will have been wasted and I'll be right back where I started. Better to not try at all."

Compounding matters, many disorganized people laden themselves with negative names: packrat, clutter bug, slob. What we don't realize is that nothing is wrong with us. It's our *systems* that aren't working.

In *Organizing for the Creative Person,* authors Dorothy Lemkuhl and Delores Cotter Lamping, C.S.W. examine and explain different functioning styles. We all think differently. Being organized is a style, like being left- or right-brained, or like being a kinesthetic, tactile, visual, or auditory learner. The book contains a brief quiz that helps identify learning styles and provides organizing techniques that work best for each style.

Organizing doesn't come naturally to everyone. Some people suffer from a lifetime of chronic disorganization. For others, precipitating events can bring on temporary bouts of disorganization. A cluttered environment can be either the cause or the effect of anxiety or depression. But anyone can learn to be more organized.

What needs to take place first, the authors explain, is the shift from "should be" to "want to be" more organized. Getting organized must be a conscious choice. With choice, one is open to change and many of the aforementioned feelings can be overcome.

Once you've chosen to get organized, reach out for help. Just as you might seek professional help from an accountant or an attorney, you can seek help from a professional organizer. A good organizer is trained to be non-judgmental, non-criticizing, supportive, and encouraging, thus reducing the fear factor.

So face the fear of bringing in a stranger, even though conditions are not ideal. There's no need to be embarrassed to see a doctor when you are ill, right? There's no need to feel embarrassed in having an organizer see your clutter, either. That's what organizers see and do everyday. It's our job. We are not visitors or company.

The simple act of inviting us in sets the ball in motion. Just as with any new challenge, the process becomes easier as you go along. Once you've tried it, you'll like it. The feelings associated with creating orderly surroundings lead to feelings of peacefulness and serenity. You will feel in control, and your life will be on an upswing.

Tips for Success

- Accept your limitations—time, space, energy, and money.

- Be consistent. Do a little at a time on an on-going basis.

- Acknowledge your successes. Success breeds success, motivating you to do more.

- Take one day at a time (to be as organized as you can be).

- Realize the only expectations you need to live up to are your own.
- If you regress, start again. Today is a new day.

CHAPTER 3
AFFLUENZA AND DISPOSAPHOBIA

Did your eyes just do a double take? Did someone misspell a couple of words? No, your eyes are seeing new words.

Affluenza is defined as a "condition of overload, debt, anxiety, and waste resulting from the dogged pursuit of more" (from *Affluenza: The All-Consuming Epidemic*). Professional organizers see the results of affluenza on a regular basis, particularly in homes that have become uncomfortably crowded, cluttered, and chaotic. Businesses are becoming equally infected as business owners fill their homes, then take the overflow to their offices and storage areas at work.

Speaking of storage, only in America do we spend millions of dollars housing our excess items in garages while parking our cars—worth tens of thousands of dollars—outdoors, exposed to the elements. And storing our belongings extends beyond our garages. According to an article in *USA Today* (December 26, 2003) self-storage units jumped 31% in one year, with one in eight U.S. households having a self-storage unit. (I'm guessing this doesn't include those people who store their clutter at work.)

How do we wind up with so many possessions that we need storage units? One answer is that we buy them. Among the symptoms of affluenza is buying things for the wrong reasons. There's spaving (spending to save): "It was on sale and

7

was too good of a bargain to pass up." There are misguided good intentions: "I may find a use for it one day." "Someone else I know may need it one day." And there's shopping as an intoxicant: "It feels good to make a purchase." (As with other drugs, this high soon wears off.)

At the same time that we are acquiring our clutter, another phenomenon comes into play—*disposaphobia*. As it sounds, this is the fear of disposing, of letting go and getting rid of things. Those of us who like to shop usually do not like to get rid of things. And so our clutter builds.

The Cure

When a business calls for professional organizing, it generally is in reference to paperwork, time management, and systems flow. More and more, though, businesses are requesting help dealing with corporate clutter. In most cases, the clutter is the personal effects of the business owner. In these cases, organizers help thin out the clutter and rearrange what remains to make the best use of the space. Housing overflow items that are not being used (and probably never will be) is an expensive use of space.

Be aware that clearing clutter and organizing takes time. Too many people call an organizer and expect that their cluttered spaces can be transformed in four hours. It took years for the cluttered condition to develop; it's not going to be eliminated in one session. Some of my professional colleagues who have been featured on the TV show "Mission: Organization" report that it took 80 to 100 hours, with the help of carpenters and support staff, to film the half-hour long episodes, and *only one room was organized*.

Simply clearing away the clutter will not get you organized. You must have a system established that will keep the clutter from accumulating again. Professional organizers customize systems to meet the needs of each individual business owner. We help you decide which items to give away, throw away, or keep. We teach you how to maintain the systems and space in the future.

A Rule To Live By

If you truly want to break the cycle of affluenza, confine your shopping to things you *need* (not just *want*) that fit the amount of space you have. Before making a purchase, answer two questions: "What am I going to use it for?" and "Where am I going to put it?" If you can't answer both questions, don't buy it!

As for curing disposaphobia, follow the organizers' rule: "One in, one out." When you buy something new, give something away. Not only will this keep clutter from building up again, but knowing that you have committed to getting rid of something can make you think twice before bringing in a new object.

DIANE A. HATCHER-CPO®

CHAPTER 4
ARE YOU CHRONICALLY DISORGANIZED?

Does your office look like a tornado just blew through? Do you spend hours looking for something you know is around here somewhere? Do you lay piles of papers anywhere you can find space, and rarely ever put them away? Do you have piles of papers all around your office, desk, and floor?

Yes? Then you might have a condition referred to in the professional organizing industry as chronic disorganization (CD). Although it's not a medical or psychological diagnosis, it can cause real problems. According to the National Study Group on Chronic Disorganization (NSGCD), of which I am a member, being chronically disorganized is officially defined by the following:

- severe disorganization over a long period of time, most of your adult life
- disorganization that adversely affects your life or that of those around you
- failed self-help efforts to get organized.

According to NSGCD, a chronically disorganized individual exhibits some or all of the following characteristics:

- accumulates large quantities of objects, documents,

papers, or possessions beyond their apparent necessity or pleasure
- has difficulty parting with things and letting go
- has a wide range of interests and many uncompleted projects
- needs visual cues to remind one to take action (leaves things laying out)
- tends to be easily distracted or loses concentration
- often has weak time-management skills.

Chronically disorganized people can make life difficult for those around them, as well as for themselves. CD people are rarely prepared for meetings or appointments, and have trouble paying bills on time, meeting deadlines, or finishing things they start. They live from one crisis to another. They may feel they have little control over their lives, that life tends to control *them*.

Can people be chronically disorganized at work and not at home, or vice versa? Yes. One reason for this can be a lack of self-discipline complicated by intimidation. As CDs get farther behind in their paperwork, clutter, and disorganization, they avoid these areas more and more. The stresses and frustrations created by their mess (such as losing items and papers) are preferable to the sense of overwhelm experienced when facing a chaotic mountain of backlog.

Disciplining one's self to get organized can be as simple as taking the time to do so. Many of the CDs I know are constantly on the run. They are too busy to take time to get organized. Ironically, taking time to organize can be one of the most valuable uses of a CD's time. Instead, their time is spent compounding the problem. While in their office, they perpetuate their disorder by stepping *over* and working *around* the piles, not realizing the stress they feel is due to their disorganized surroundings and their inability to locate things easily.

If you are CD and have been too busy to get organized, think about simplifying your life. Being busy may suit you, but it can actually result in a loss of productivity if you are not organized. Commit to putting in a few hours at a time to get organized. Find a home for each item. Discipline yourself to put new papers and items away when you bring them into the office.

You will be guaranteed to reap the rewards of your efforts. When you are organized, you have more time for such proactive projects as providing customer service, sales and marketing efforts, and spending time with your employees. With that additional time, you acquire the peace of mind to enjoy business meetings, lunches, and maybe even an occasional round of golf.

Soon you will be on your way to a new-found sense of freedom and control when you are in your office. You will then begin to notice how it's positively affecting other areas of your life as well.

DIANE A. HATCHER-CPO®

CHAPTER 5
PROCRASTINATION IN THE OFFICE

I had been meaning to write this chapter sooner, but... I couldn't get motivated. I was afraid it wouldn't come out right. I was tired. I really didn't feel well. Some friends dropped by. I was too busy. My house needed cleaning. I really wanted to do something more fun. Ever hear yourself saying similar things when you have a task you need to complete? Certainly, everyone has, even me, but I employ methods that work for me to get through it.

If you are a procrastinator, sometimes changing the habit can be as simple as sitting down and exploring your thought processes. Next time you find yourself procrastinating, use these steps to think it through. Ask yourself, "Why don't I want to do it now? Is it boring? Overwhelming? Do I only have small blocks of time available, yet I want to do everything from start to finish in one sitting? Am I tired? Do I fear failing or that it won't turn out perfectly?"

Each of these questions leads to a different conclusion and can be dealt with in its own way. For instance, if it seems boring, but you know it needs to be done, do it anyway. Consider the consequences if you don't do it.

If it feels overwhelming, break it down into smaller parts and do one or several parts at a time. Then take a break, or do more small parts the next time you have time.

If you have only small blocks of time available, make this a *good* thing. First change your mindset that it all has to get done at once, because it doesn't. That's just a belief you have that is interfering with your progress. Small blocks of time mean you only need to do a small amount of work.

Are you tired? Be aware of your circadian rhythms. Each of us peaks at different hours of the day. If you are more energetic and alert in the mornings, choose that time to tackle a situation over which you are procrastinating. Most of us have low periods of energy just before and after lunch. Be aware of this and don't try to tackle large projects at those times. Before and after lunch is usually a good time to catch up on mundane activities such as filing or opening mail.

Is your procrastination based in fear? Are you afraid of losing things, forgetting things, not finishing things, doing the wrong thing, failing? Giving in to these fears just makes your life harder because what needs doing isn't getting done. This lack of action generally affects others and, in turn, can affect your self-esteem, relationships, and possibly your job security.

Deadlines

When is your project due? Whatever your deadline, write it in your planner or on your calendar *several days prior to the actual due date*. Even though intellectually you'll know the real date, seeing it in writing spurs you to action. Writing it down also gives it validity in your mind.

Some deadlines are self-imposed. For example, do you hate writing thank you notes? Many people do. Although experts maintain that it's best to send them within a week of an occurrence, no one is monitoring that you actually do so. Again, think it through. What is the purpose of a thank you note? You know your client will appreciate it. You know it gets your name out in front of him again for next-to-no expense or effort. By seeing your name while he is still feeling good about your work, he is likely to recommend you to others. Your timeliness and consideration will impress him. Therein lies the motivation to get it done.

More Suggestions for Success

If you are easily distracted, keep only one project on your desk at a time to minimize distractions. Make a plan and stick to it. Give yourself a time span to spend on parts of the project, then don't stray from your plan. While you are accomplishing this goal, focus on it. Don't let your mind be thinking about something else.

Try setting smaller goals, then rewarding yourself as you make progress. After all, small successes add up and tend to motivate you further. A reward can be as simple as having a cup of your favorite coffee, phoning a friend, or going for a walk in the park. Only you know what is rewarding to you.

Finally, another question to explore before giving in to the temptation of avoidance is: "How will I feel when this is done?" Most likely you will feel a sense of completion, possibly pride, and stress relief. That's a big one for me. Getting things done and crossed off my list feels liberating and hugely satisfying.

People procrastinate for many reasons that I have not touched on here, and there are many more techniques that can be applied to get you through them. Use this chapter as a starting place. These methods work and can help you feel more successful. It takes a bit of discipline but, hey, that's why we are procrastinating in the first place!

CHAPTER 6
IT'S NOT ABOUT PERFECTION

When people meet me for the first time, they often say, "I wish I could see *your* house," or "I'd love to see *your* desk." Apparently, some people think organizing is about perfection. But being perfectly organized is unrealistic. Presuming that my desk, house, or self would be perfect is an unfair assumption. Equating organization with perfection also limits these people's ability to reach out for help. Since perfection is impossible to achieve, they rationalize, being organized must be impossible, too, so why bother working with a professional organizer?

A professional organizer's goal is not to get you "perfectly" organized. On the contrary, we help you get organized "enough." What does "organized enough" look like to you? Think about what interferes most with your quality of life or your relationships. What causes you the most stress? What would you like to have eliminated and replaced by useful systems? Professional organizers can help you remove these sources of stress and create functioning systems. We devise solutions based on your needs, not ours. Organizing is about making your life work more smoothly, not about perfection.

Form Follows Function

For many years, I could not understand the phrase "form follows function," which is used repeatedly in the interior design/decorating business. As a result of helping hundreds of clients to become organized, though, I have come to understand the concept.

A frequent misconception is that being organized is foremost about appearance and neatness. It's true that, once your environment is organized, it appears neater. But being organized is no more about neatness first than it is about being perfect. Organization creates efficiency and effectiveness, making your life and surroundings work optimally for you. That is the *function* of being organized. The *form* of our environment—the tidy appearance—is a *consequence* of being organized. Hence the phrase "form *follows* function."

After organizing your papers and things, your space will be more visually appealing. This is why professional organizers are able to work closely with interior designers and decorators, re-designers, feng shui practitioners, and closet-system specialists. We are all interested in improving your environment, focusing on function first, then form.

Staying Organized

A third misconception about being organized is that it's a one-time activity with an end. People mistakenly think that, once they've gotten everything organized, it will stay that way forever. But this is rarely true.

Organizing is a process, not a destination. It's an ever-evolving process that ebbs and flows with the changes in your life. Your work sessions on an organizing project with a professional organizer may come to an end, but your life continues. Events such as depression, a recent marriage, divorce, birth, a family death, a job change, etc. can temporarily inhibit your ability or desire to be detail-oriented and work your organizing systems, thus causing them to break down. After all, as John Lennon said, "Life is what happens to you while you're busy making other plans."

A professional organizer can help you cut through the clutter and organize your time, space, and things, developing the most appropriate solutions suited to your needs and style. This ensures a better chance that you'll use and maintain the systems, and stay organized. And when your life interferes, your systems make it much easier to recoup what was working and jump back on track.

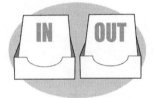

DIANE A. HATCHER-CPO®

CHAPTER 7
THE COST OF CORPORATE CLUTTER

I s it any coincidence that so many successful business people are organized? Since success equals profits, it follows that organization equals profits. When you are organized, your time is spent constructively on activities pertinent to your business, including sales, marketing, networking, and customer relations.

If organization equals profits, disorganization results in unnecessary costs. When you are disorganized, you lose time searching for misplaced items. (The *Wall Street Journal* reports that the average American business person loses six weeks each year searching for lost items.) You miss deadlines and appointments, tarnishing your reputation and possibly losing business. You pay bills late, incurring late fees. You request an extension on your taxes, generating a penalty fee. These complications cause stress, embarrassment, general inefficiency, a loss of productivity and, most likely, a reduction in profits.

Beating the Battle of the (Paper) Bulge

A primary factor in workplace disorganization is clutter, of which paper is hands-down the biggest source. Consider these interesting statistics. Then consider which papers you are saving and what saving them is costing you. What time and resources could you save?

- Even with e-mail and digital storage, the volume of paper has increased 100% since 1995.
- 90% of information is still on paper.
- We use only 20% of the paper we keep.
- In U.S. offices, paper consumption jumped 12% between 1995 and 2000, *even while computer usage increased by 5%*. This is because we prefer to read information on paper. Even with advances in the visual quality of computer monitors, we continue to print out e-mail attachments.

To win the war on your burgeoning piles of paper, you'll need to consciously decide to keep or toss every piece of paper you acquire. Consider the document's creation date. Is it still relevant, and does it contain the most recent information? More importantly, what would be the worst consequence if you threw it away? If not having the document would be a showstopper, keep it. If it can be replicated or done without, toss it. This decision-making process should be employed for each document as soon as possible after it hits your desk or in-basket. With practice, this process becomes a habit and can be employed rather quickly.

And Then There is E-Mail

E-mail is another form of clutter. It has increased logarithmically as an official method of business communication. However, it's usually created, distributed, filed, and destroyed informally and in ways that regular paper documents are not. Most employees don't take the time to manage their e-mail documents properly.

Here are some more statistics:

- By 2005, an estimated 225 million e-mail boxes were in use by organizations worldwide.
- 93% of businesses use e-mail to respond to customer inquiries, 84% for discussing strategy, 82% for filing or responding to regulatory requirements, and 71% for negotiating contracts.
- 93% of business information is in digital form.
- 35% to 60% of business-critical information is stored in personal messaging systems.
- A typical business person spends just over two hours using e-mail each day and 40 minutes of that time managing it.
- 53% of business people check e-mail at least six times a day.
- 4% of business people check e-mail constantly throughout the day.

According to the American Records Management Association, problems that can be caused by disorganized use of computers and other technology include:

- **Lost time.** 7.3% of work time is spent finding misplaced files.
- **Lost information.** 3 to 5% of all files are lost, at a cost of $180 per document to recreate.
- **Lost business.** As a result of lost or mismanaged files, an organization will lose future business. For example: A Fortune 1000 company, which manages one million files using technology, will lose $5 million in business.

To manage e-mail more effectively, use the same principles

as you would for paper management. Decide what action to take on the e-mail while it's still in your in-box, and either act on it, file it, or delete it. For fewer distractions to your business day, mute your computer's volume control so you are not aware of each e-mail's arrival. Limit yourself to certain times of the day and implement a specific time limit for checking and managing e-mail.

(My thanks to Karen McFarland Payne, CRM, owner of Precision Organizing and Records Management, LLC for sharing the information in this chapter. Karen is a Certified Records Manager and a professional organizer in Milwaukee, Wisconsin. She can be contacted at Karen@precisionorganizing.com or by visiting www.precisionorganizing.com.)

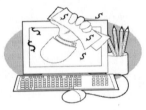

CHAPTER 8
RIDING THE RAFT TO SUCCESS

Are you drowning in a sea of papers? Well hop aboard, because this life-preserving RAFT is sailing away and taking your papers with it.

Planning Your Journey

In 1998, I copyrighted the RAFT Organizing System. Since then, it has entered the mainstream, having appeared on television shows and in articles by other organizers. They say that imitation is the highest form of flattery; clearly, RAFT has been endorsed as a system that works!

I developed the RAFT system to provide direction and simplify decision-making for paper that crosses your desk. The theory behind RAFT is that every piece of paper you touch can fall into one of the following categories:

R— Read or Refer
A—Act
F—File
T—Toss

OHIO (Only Handle It Once), is a popular acronym and, in some cases, it's applicable. For example, incoming mail that can be handled in 60 seconds or less should be handled right away. But the truth is that most paper can't be fully processed the first time you pick it up. Still, you can keep from shuffling papers from one pile to another by using the RAFT system. Here's what you do. The first time you handle a paper, determine what the next action is that needs to be taken for that paper. The action will be one of only five choices: read, refer, act, file, or toss.

A paper fits into the Read category if it needs to be read for information purposes only. No other action is required on it. A good example would be a list of organizing tips.

Refer, the other "R" choice, would be for paper that someone else should see or can handle. It can be something to delegate or something to share with a colleague. For instance, when you are separating mail, you may get mail for other people in your office. So you need a designated spot to hold it until you can give it to them. (Most one-person offices do not need a Refer category.)

A paper falls into the Act category if it requires a *decision,* a *response,* or has a *deadline* associated with it. It may be necessary to create sub-categories for some of these actions. Examples of Act sub-categories include "people to call," "computer research," "letters to write," etc. Note: one major activity that should never go into the Act category is "bills to pay." A separate file or a tickler system needs to be established for the bills to pay.

A paper belongs in the File category when you are finished actively working with it and you know you need to keep it for possible reference in the future. I will discuss setting up a filing system in Chapter 10. For now, know that papers with which you are still working should never be placed in your file drawer.

"Toss" means the paper has no reason to stay in your office. It will never ride your RAFT; instead, it goes directly to the trash. (I love this category the most. Learn to welcome it, and treasure it if you are a packrat.)

Building Your RAFT

In order for papers to be plucked from the sea and RAFTed away, they must have a temporary home, a place to go after you have designated their RAFT category. This entails creating an *activity center.*

Obtain five stacking trays, also known as letter trays, and stack four of them, one over the other. (They are designed to interlock this way.) Whether you use letter or legal size is a personal preference. Most industries have moved away from legal size paper, making it unnecessary.

Label the top three trays to contain their RAFT parts: Act, Read, and File. (I recommend that you label the trays To Do, To Read, and To File because it reminds you that you need to take action.) Labeling is important; it saves you time and makes the system easier to use down the line.

Notice that the Refer tray is not one of the stacked trays. Instead, locate it in an area on the way out of your office, such as at the edge of your desk. When you are leaving your office, take the papers with you to distribute to the appropriate people.

The bottom tray can be labeled Miscellaneous. This tray holds frequently accessed papers such as fax cover sheets, letterhead stationery, current week's receipts, a company phone list, etc. If you are liable to put items in this tray because you don't know where on the RAFT they belong, *do not* give yourself a Miscellaneous tray. This is not what it's for. If you are having difficulty determining which category to place the paper in, review the RAFT definitions above.

All Aboard Your RAFT

Now you are ready to clean up that sea of papers (i.e. backlog) once and for all. Wade in and gather together the papers from your desk, around your office, the floor, the incoming mail area, and wherever else they've set down anchor. Starting with the most recent, sort them into their corresponding RAFT category trays.

Don't forget to toss items overboard into your trash can. Toss anything that is not tax-related, is out of date, is junk mail or an offer you didn't request, or is a copy of something that is elsewhere in the office. Be ruthless. Don't save things "just because, maybe one day, someday, if..." It's not worth it. If you can't think of a specific reason to keep something, don't. (On the other hand, if it brings up an emotional response in you, or your intuition tells you it needs to be kept, err on the side of caution and keep it.)

This portion of your journey could take a while. You may need to divide the trip into ports of call. Travel a little, do some other work, take a break, come back to your RAFT, then travel some more. Don't forget to visit the sticky notes on your wall and computer, and any other loose papers during your journey. Before you know it, your seas will be clear for smooth sailing and all your paperwork will be neatly stacked into the four trays that make up your activity center.

Enjoying the Ride

Remember I mentioned earlier that your papers were in *temporary* homes? They live in their trays until you take them out to perform the applicable actions: reading, filing, making calls, doing computer research, copying or faxing, etc. This is where much of your work comes from during your workday.

When the mail arrives each day, sort it into your RAFT trays. Do not, however, RAFT away the items that you will be working on today. Today's tasks remain in a single stack on your desk, easily accessible.

At the end of each day, search the To Do tray for items that need to be handled the next day. Papers, files, and projects—anything with an impending deadline—can be taken out of the tray and added neatly to the stack on your desk.

Also at the end of each day, clear your desk by sorting papers back into their appropriate trays. However, leave out anything that you plan to work on the next day. Keep these items in your Today's Tasks stack.

Using this system, you'll find that your journeys on the sea of paper will be much shorter, and you will be RAFTed to your destination with less stress and frustration. You will look and feel organized. Smooth sailing!

DIANE A. HATCHER-CPO®

CHAPTER 9
6 EASY STEPS TO REDUCING PAPER

The advent of computers promised us a paperless society. Instead, our paper production has increased. We print out e-mails, make multiple copies on the copy machine, and send and receive faxes with the touch of a button. However, we can keep our paper under control with these six simple steps.

1. **Don't allow papers to build up.** Handle paper on a daily basis. Open mail daily. If you let it grow into a pile for days or weeks, it gets out of control and more difficult to deal with.

2. **Make a decision on each paper the first time you touch it.** This doesn't mean that every time you get a sheet of paper that you have to work on it immediately. It simply means that, rather than putting it down somewhere temporary —like on the dining room table or a desk—you have a plan for it. If it can be completed in 60 seconds or less, do it now. Otherwise, use your RAFT system, putting it into trays to be worked on at a more appropriate time.

3. **Follow through on the work.** Avoid shuffling— moving paper from your in-box to your desk to your table, into your action tray and back to your desk. Instead, each time you pick up a sheet of paper, make a small dot in the upper right hand corner. Notice anything? You may be procrastinating.

Three or more dots indicate that it's past time to take action on that paper. Refer back to Step 2.

4. Be ruthless. 80% of what is filed is never accessed again, so 80% or more of the paper you receive on a daily basis can be immediately discarded. Keep a garbage can or recycle bin within reach when opening mail. Go through your in-box each day and toss anything that doesn't concern you. Remove yourself from distribution lists and magazine subscriptions you don't need. Purge your files once or twice a year at least.

5. Think before you print. Do you really need to print every single e-mail you get? Many e-mails, once read, can immediately be deleted. If you have to keep an e-mail, create folders for storing them on the computer. If you must print an e-mail or a Web page, decide if you really need to print the entire thing. You can highlight a portion of an e-mail or a Web site with your mouse, then click on File, Print, then choose Print Selection. This prints only the portion you need.

6. Follow retention guidelines. Your company or personal accountant probably has retention guidelines specifying how long a particular paper or file must be kept. You can also obtain guidelines yourself on the Web. Using the guidelines of your choice, remove closed or inactive files from your active work drawers and place them in storage. Always indicate a "destroy" date on the box or page to ease the future purging process. Purging outdated files provides more space for the coming year's papers. Space can be re-used rather than adding new filing cabinets.

While we may never become a truly paperless society, following these six steps will help keep your sea of paper from getting too choppy. And calm waters make for a gentler ride in your RAFT!

DIANE A. HATCHER-CPO®

CHAPTER 10
FILING 101 FOR SMARTIES

Raise your hand if you like filing.

I thought so. Filing is one of those necessary evils we avoid as "not a priority," yet when it piles up and must be done, it's an agony. So let's look at some ways that filing can be a little more pleasant. Then we can appreciate it for the value it really holds.

Setting up your filing system properly is key. When items are easily retrieved, you save time and eliminate stress from a mundane activity.

There are different ways to set up your filing system. Two alphabetical systems are possible. One is straight alphabetical, like the white pages in a phone book. The other is to alphabetize by categories, like the yellow pages in a phone book. Some systems use categories with colored hanging files, others use identification numbers in place of clients' names, while others are chronological. The method you choose will depend on your needs as well as other circumstances specific to your industry.

For home offices, keep business and personal filing systems separate. Have one cabinet or drawer just for your business and another for your personal files. This, too, makes filing and retrieval easier.

Equipping Your Drawers

Most desks have a large bottom drawer. Use that drawer

for files that need to be accessed often. It helps if the files face you as you sit at your desk. Some drawers have bars that can be reconfigured in order to face the files toward you (sideways, i.e. perpendicular, from the front of the drawer).

Use hanging files to hold one or more file folders. Hanging files mark your place when you remove a file and keep file folders upright so they won't slide down under other files in the drawer, never to be found again.

Hanging files and file folders come in two sizes, letter-size for 8.5" x 11" papers, and legal-size for 8.5" x 14" papers. If the majority of what you handle is 8.5" x 11", use letter size. It's less cumbersome and saves drawer space and money.

Don't overload your files. A maximum thickness of one inch for file folders and two inches for hanging files is a good rule of thumb.

Consider using colored hanging files and file folders. Studies show that color-coding your system can reduce the time it takes to find a file by 50%. For example, use red files for insurance records, yellow for vacation files, and green for investments to make visual identification easier. Instead of colored files, you can use color-coded file tabs or gummed labels with a pre-printed color stripe.

Tips for Buying a Filing Cabinet

When purchasing a filing cabinet, look for one that is sturdy and has drawers that work smoothly. Make sure you can pull out the drawers all the way to easily access files, and that the cabinet doesn't tip over when the top drawer is opened or full.

Another desirable feature to look for is high-sided drawers that are designed to hold hanging files without having to add a frame. If this isn't part of the filing cabinet, a drawer frame can be bought separately and installed. Although not a complex procedure, it requires some extra work and can be unstable.

Spraying a silicone lubricant once a year on the tracks will keep the drawers functioning smoothly and quietly.

Use Your Cabinet

If possible, file daily, or at least once a week. File at a low-energy period in your day, such as just before or after lunch, or at the end of the day on Friday. The advantage to filing on Friday is that, on Monday, you come back to a clean, organized office—fresh, energized, and ready for work.

Garbage In, Garbage Out

"Garbage in, garbage out" was a widely used phrase in the early days of personal computers. The idea was that computers were only as good as the information that was fed to them. Our files work (or not) on the same concept. If they are crammed full of useless information, they will be difficult to use and of little value.

Many people neglect their filing cabinets until they run out of space. When their drawers are too full and they can fit nothing else, they buy a new filing cabinet. When space prohibits more cabinets, panic sets in.

The organizing industry recommends purging files at least once a year, especially at year's end. This provides room in your active files for the coming year. Even if it's not the end of the year, if your files are feeling tight or looking full in the drawers, it's time to purge.

The first order of purging is to throw away anything that is a duplicate, out-dated, or can be found elsewhere, such as online. Look online or ask your tax advisor for retention guidelines to help you determine how long to hold onto necessary items. Obtain these from several sources because some tend to contradict one another. (You can Google "retention guidelines" for a choice of sources.) When faced with contradictory information, choose the longest retention period. If you are uncomfortable following the retention guidelines, list any particular areas of concern, then ask your financial advisor or accountant about them. They can advise what is best for your particular situation.

Get Going

If you have not purged annually, prepare for a tedious, long haul the first time you attack this situation. Schedule time to get going. Work for short periods at first. Plan to work for an hour once a week, or just do one drawer, then stop until next time. Or do 25 files, then take a break. Whatever it takes to keep you motivated and moving, do what works. Try increasing your time a little during the next session. You will be surprised what mental and emotional freedom you feel once you start purging!

Set up an archive box or drawer for those papers the retention guides indicate should be saved. Rather than keeping all your previous tax returns and supporting documentation in your active drawer, move them to the archive file or box so only current items remain in your office files. Pull any other "save us" items from the active files and place them in the archive area, too. (In general, anything within the current year can be considered active, and previous years, inactive.)

To reduce the workload of future purges, refer to your retention guidelines *before* filing. Ask yourself, "Am I likely to use this in the future and, if so, for what? Could I obtain a copy somewhere else if needed? What would be the worst thing that could happen if I do not save it? Will I be able to find it if I need it in the distant future?" Your answers will help you decide whether to keep it. The more you keep, the more difficult it is to locate the things you do need, the more space it requires, and the more time-consuming it will be to purge.

One more thing. While purging, avoid thoroughly reading the content of each paper. Quickly scan to find the information you need to decide whether or not to toss it, then move on. Otherwise, you will become easily distracted and never finish.

DIANE A. HATCHER-CPO®

CHAPTER 11
ORGANIZING THOSE PESKY RECEIPTS

How much money is your accountant charging you to organize your receipts? Or, if your accountant expects you to organize your receipts before coming in at tax time, how much time and money are *you* spending to put your receipts in order? Compute the value of your hourly rate and multiply it by the number of hours you spend organizing your receipts. Wouldn't you rather spend your time being productive or relaxing?

Three issues must be addressed to organize receipts: knowing which receipts you need to keep; knowing where to keep them; and being able to retrieve them easily if needed. Does your system for dealing with receipts address these issues? (I'm not talking about the shoe box method. Throwing all your receipts into a box or envelope only resolves the second issue, and complicates the third.) Let's look at each of these three issues, one step at a time.

Which Receipts Do You Need To Keep?

- All receipts associated with income tax documentation, including charitable donations.
- All business-related receipts (including utilities if applicable).
- Items that may need to be returned. Toss the receipts when the return date passes.

- Items paid for with a credit or debit card. When your statement comes, match up the receipts. Contact the bank to resolve any disputes. You can then throw out the receipts.
- Large purchases that have warranties.
- Paid utility bills, until next month's arrives. Or save them for one year, then purge all but December's to start the new year.
- For investment reports, *always* keep the initial opening statement and year-end annual summaries. Quarterly reports can be kept for the year, then shredded when the annual summary arrives.
- Consult your tax professional, financial adviser, or attorney regarding financial and legal papers.

Where Do You Keep Them?

There are several workable systems, so choose the one below that suits your style. (If you claim business expenses, set up a second system. Never mix business and personal.)

- Get a monthly-labeled accordion file and maintain it based on the preceding guidelines. The accordion file fits comfortably in a file drawer.
- Another method is to label envelopes by month and insert receipts daily, newest ones in front. Keep the current month's envelope in a convenient, consistent place. At month's end, store the filled envelopes in file folders chronologically in your file drawer.
- An alternate method is to file saved receipts, paid bills, and invoices alphabetically by name of the company you paid (for example, Macy's, MasterCard,

etc.). Again, always place the most current ones in front so they remain in chronological order.

- A fourth method is to purchase a bill-paying kit, available from catalogs or online. Consult their instructions.

- With each of these systems, create a "tax" section to store proof of donations and other tax-deductible receipts together.

- For large purchases and/or electronics with manuals and warranties, staple the receipt inside the manual. File the manual in an A to Z accordion file.

- For business, it's important to file receipts in categories based on Schedule C, which lists deductible expenses. The exception to this is if you are using accounting software, in which case receipts can be filed by month as they will cross-reference with your accounting system should you need to locate a particular receipt.

How Do You Find Them?

What was previously difficult is now easy.

- If filed monthly, figure out approximately which month the item was purchased. Items purchased later in the month will be toward the front of the envelope or monthly divider; receipts acquired early in the month will be toward the back.

- If filed alphabetically, locate the file of the company you paid. The receipts will be in chronological order by date within the correct alphabetical listing.

Maintenance

Organize your receipts as you get them by placing them immediately into the designated system, preferably on a daily basis. Small tasks are easier to accomplish than a huge, time-consuming (dreaded) project.

In order to keep this system operable from year to year, you'll need to purge annually (usually at the end of the year). Pull the previous year's receipts and relocate them to an archive, or inactive, filing container (such as a plastic bin or filing drawer). Separate out the receipts you'll need for taxes and put them in a tax file for that year. Once you've emptied the files/ envelopes of last year's receipts, you can re-use the files for the upcoming year. There's no need to buy more filing cabinets or filing supplies.

Another issue altogether is how long to keep a receipt. When in doubt, *don't* throw it out. Instead, surf the Internet for retention schedules (see Chapter 9) and ask your financial experts for guidance.

CHAPTER 12
FUN WITH OFFICE SUPPLIES

Office supplies *can* be fun. You know how a new rug in the bathroom, a new lamp in the living room, or new dishes in the kitchen can spruce up your home? Well, there are plenty of little items that can do the same for your office. Eventually you may want to call in an interior designer to decorate, or bring in a professional organizer to make your office more functional. Until then, browse through the inventory at your local office supplier and pick up a combination of the following supplies, just for fun.

Play with Color

- Gold paper clips give your papers a classy look and reflect your good taste.
- Colored staples are bright, plastic coated, and rust resistant.
- Pens come in a multitude of colors and styles. One fun pen option is gel, a soft, pastel-colored ink that writes on dark blue or black paper.
- Sticky notes are available in bright neon colors, pastels, and dark blue or black, lined and unlined. No need to be bored with that original pale yellow any longer. Write on the dark ones with gel pens for a contemporary new look.
- Lucite, see-through colored phones are available

in blue, teal, red, violet, and clear. These can be combined with matching Lucite-looking answering machines and Caller-ID stations.

- Colored file folders can be functional as well as cheerful. To save time, try using a purple folder for Pending items, a green file for Bills to Pay, and an orange file for Upcoming Events. Because the colored file stands out, it's easily located on your busy desk.
- Stacking trays, pencil holders, and note pad holders remain available in traditional wood tones such as mahogany, cherry, and oak, You can also get them in glass, Lucite, or molded plastic, in such colors as burgundy, white, black, clear, and gold. For a contemporary look, try silver, black, or purple mesh metals, or designer-inspired styles.

Add Art

Walls don't need to be bare or traditional. Check out motivational posters and colorful theme calendars displaying your favorite hobbies or interests. Or pick up some inexpensive prints of your favorite paintings and have them framed. Explore different kinds of frames; they can add pizzazz while reflecting your personal style.

Don't forget a couple (but no more) family photos on your desk. Photos of family, pets, and other loved ones can also sit on shelves or file cabinets, or be hung on walls. During a long day when you're feeling overwhelmed, tired, or stressed, pause a moment to enjoy looking at your favorite photos.

Add Humor

Think your planner has to be plain and dull? Think again.

Planners now come with Far Side cartoons, golf course scenes, travel backgrounds, and more. Traditional leather or pastel colors add interest to your desk and reflect your individuality.

Put your office guests in a good mood with a candy jar full of bite-sized chocolates, wrapped hard candies, or colorful gumballs. Locate the jar on the edge of your desk or on a small table near their chairs.

If it doesn't clash with your surroundings, a bulletin board can brighten up your day. Neatly decorate the bulletin board with inspirational sayings, (tasteful) jokes, and images that make you smile.

I could continue on about clipboards, scissors, and the like, but it will be much more fun if you review the next office catalog that crosses your desk or visit your local office supply store soon. Happy surroundings!

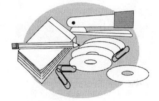

CHAPTER 13
ORGANIZING THE OFFICE
SUPPLY CABINET

I t's great to stock fun office supplies. Storing them is another issue altogether.

Tired of not being able to find things when she needed them, Linda (not her real name), a busy immigration attorney, decided she needed an office overhaul. This included tackling her office supply cabinet.

This was not Linda's first session with me. We had worked together on and off for a period of three years. In previous sessions we attended to some crisis organizing issues, such as time management and cataloging files for off-site storage, but we never got to the supply cabinet. One day, while in her office indexing and packing closed files, I noticed the overflowing cabinet.

"It's amazing how something so nondescript as a supply cabinet can contribute to the overall disorganization of the flow of the office," Linda remarked after I broached the subject.

I commented on the amount of time that must get wasted whenever someone needed to retrieve an item from that closet. "That's the problem," said Linda. "Whenever I send someone over there to get me a mailing envelope or a computer ink cartridge, it seems like they must get lost, judging from the length of time it takes them to return."

The Problem

Linda's office supply cabinet had neither rhyme nor reason to its shelves and the items on them. Three shelves contained envelopes falling down and, in some cases, getting bent. Cleaning products were on the prime-space shelves (the ones at eye level, which can easily be reached). Office supplies were crammed in wherever they could fit, and an eight-inch-high pile of index-tabbed pages teetered on the bottom shelf.

Linda's cabinet had become a dumping ground, often used, easily ignored. Everyone in the office was busy with her own job, and no one had been assigned responsibility for maintaining the cabinet; therefore, the lowly office supply cabinet declined into disarray.

Getting It Organized

Usually I prefer to work side by side with clients, getting their input as I go along. In the case of Linda's office supply cabinet, however, I was able to work more independently, saving up questions. Linda and her employees continued at their jobs as I tackled the cabinet, interrupted every so often by someone coming into the room to retrieve a supply. By then I usually had a question. In some cases, I was surprised that only Linda knew the answer.

Among other things, I noticed an abundance of air freight envelopes. It turned out that the firm no longer even used one of the companies, so that stack was tossed out. (Tossing, with the client's approval, is my favorite activity. It creates space, providing room for the items being kept). We designated the top shelf as the only shelf to be used for DHL, FedEx, and USPS envelopes of varying sizes because the majority of those envelopes started there. (There's no sense in moving something if it works where it is). The envelopes were then sorted and combined with those from other shelves.

On the second shelf, we housed the small general office supplies, including paper clips, staples, pens, tape, and markers. Continuing with the organizing rule that instructs us to group similar items together, we placed all computer-related supplies (floppy disks, labels, ink cartridges, CDs) on one side of the third shelf. The other side of that shelf held banking supplies and reams of colored paper.

We discovered that the eight-inch-high pile of index-tabbed pages were due to employees opening a new set of tabs for each new client file and only using part of the set. Realizing that the partial sets could be combined to make full sets again (reducing the need to purchase new ones), a staff member was assigned this project. The index pages and the cleaning products (window cleaner, furniture polish, air freshener) were stored on the bottom shelf. (The cleaning products were put here because they are heavy items that might get knocked over or spill on other items below.)

Messy vs. Methodical

Some organizers prefer to start by removing all the contents, sorting them outside the cabinet, then deciding on which shelf to place them. I never do that. For one, the space I had to work in was cramped and needed to be kept open to foot traffic. Secondly, dealing with the entire lot of supplies at once can be overwhelming even for an experienced organizer. Additionally, a job might take longer than anticipated or the client might need to stop before the job is completed. In those circumstances having everything out creates chaos.

Instead I prefer to focus on one shelf at a time, starting

from the top and working down while maintaining whatever systems may already be in place (such as keeping the envelopes where they mostly already were, on the top shelf).

Mission Accomplished

In less than an hour, the cabinet had more room. Its contents were in plain sight, neat in appearance and easily retrievable. Everyone in the office was familiar with the items stored there.

In awe of what they saw, the staff wondered how this feat had been accomplished. They were bubbly and energized, as if a new piece of furniture had been added to the office. "You are amazing," one stated. "No kidding," responded another as I blushed and beamed, acknowledging their appreciation.

We discussed who would be responsible for placing new or replacement items into the cabinet in the future. While meeting with Linda's staff and giving them a brief tour of the cabinet, I reminded them to place incoming supplies near items of a similar nature. If anyone saw something out of place, they were to take a moment and fix it. In this way, the entire staff would cooperate to maintain the cabinet. Linda has since designated one person to be in charge of the supplies overall.

The significance of this story? You, too, can have an organized office supply closet with minimal effort and great results. It's worth it.

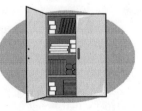

CHAPTER 14
PRACTICAL TIPS FOR SAVING TIME
AT WORK

We feel strapped for time, yet many of us fill our days with time *stealers*. In this chapter, I offer some time-saving suggestions. Some might be new to you; others might be ideas you never made the effort to implement.

Yes, I said effort. You know the saying, "No pain, no gain." Or, "It takes money to make money." Or even, "You get out of it what you put into it." But don't panic; instead, consider that "10 minutes spent planning saves 30 minutes in execution." By investing time up front, you save time in the long run. Remember what happens when you don't get preventive maintenance done on your car? You end up with larger, more-expensive problems down the line. The effort it takes to get an oil change or a tune-up when it initially comes due is minimal in comparison. The same is true with office work. Small initial investments make work easier down the road. So start with these tips, and see how well they work for you.

Answer routine letters on the original letter. This is acceptable for informal communication. When someone sends you a request that requires a response, simply hand-write a brief response on the document you received, slip it into an envelope, and mail it right back to the sender. If necessary, make a copy before you send it.

Use window envelopes. This might involve reformatting your letters. But once this initial work is done, all your letters will be aligned so the recipient's name and address shows through the window in the envelope when the letter is folded in thirds. In this way, you avoid the further step of printing out labels or hand-writing an address (which takes more time and may not look as professional).

Stop piling. Remember the saying, "Files, not piles." Set your desk and filing system up so there is a place for everything *except* piles. Piles of paper are an inefficient way to work, and are one of the greatest causes of time lost to searching for misplaced items. If you are a piler, in order to reduce and eliminate the pile, work your way from its bottom, up.

Pick up daily. Is your office in disarray? Break the habit of just laying stuff down anywhere there's space. Put it away where it belongs, every day. This is really the "secret" to keeping your office organized. Remember, taking a little time up front avoids hours of extra work later.

Purge files annually. Set a date to do so on your calendar. Go through each file and toss out papers you no longer need or for which you have duplicates. Remove any files that can be stored, such as inactive files. This keeps your files manageable, filed items easier to locate, and your file drawers more spacious and easier to use. Remember, it's never too late in the year to purge.

Take it with you. You know that stack of reading you've been meaning to get to? Each day when you are going out, take a few of those items with you to read during down times (while stuck in traffic, waiting for an appointment, in the drive-through lane at the bank or while watching TV at night). These days, many business people report that they don't have enough time to read through everything that crosses their desks. You'll be surprised at how much reading you can accomplish in bits and pieces. It's an efficient use of otherwise unproductive time, and it helps clean off your desk.

Make a copy. Along the same lines, copy articles you want to read. You don't need to carry an entire manual. When it comes to magazines or business newspapers, pull out the pages you want to read so you can take them with you easily, and discard the remainder of the publication when you are done with it.

Mark the spot. If it pains you to tear up a magazine, review the table of contents and mark the pages you'd like to read with sticky notes. This makes the articles easy to locate, so that you don't waste time flipping through pages. When done, donate the magazine to a charity, a hospital, or a nursing home, or pass it on to a co-worker or the office library.

Throw out boxes when the warranties expire. Boxes are worthless once the warranty expires and, in the case of software, once the box is opened. These boxes become another source of clutter and take up valuable storage space. Most people aren't even aware they still have these boxes until they clean out their closets and find them buried. (If you must keep a box, flatten it.)

Practice the one in, one out rule. When purchasing new business clothes, sell or donate an equal number of clothes that you haven't worn in years. This assures your clothes will always be relatively in style, and you won't find yourself embarrassed in the middle of a meeting when you suddenly realize you're wearing the pants with the worn-looking knee. It also provides closet space so your clothes are not crammed too tightly, needing ironing before you wear them each time.

Another benefit to purging your older clothing is the amount of time saved sorting through your closet, trying to decide what to wear each day.

Write it down. Forget to do things? Write it down as soon as you think of it. Always keep your To Do list, planner, or PDA (such as a Palm Pilot) easily accessible. For more on To Do lists, read the next chapter!

CHAPTER 15
THE SECRET TO TIME MANAGEMENT

Toby Keith's hit, "My List," was the number-one country song in 2002. Not coincidentally, whenever an interviewer asks me for my number-one tip to get organized, I respond "Make a daily To Do list."

Studies show that getting organized is the number-two goal behind losing weight for women, and number three overall for men and women combined. If getting organized is such a high priority, why do To Do lists fail? Underlying problems include:

- feeling as though *To Do* means *should, must,* or *have to*
- trying to start your day by writing the list
- believing it takes too long or wastes time to write the list
- believing that lists or calendars don't work
- not knowing how to write it, what items to include
- including too many tasks
- confusing a *daily* list with a *master* list
- not looking at the list often enough or losing it
- underestimating the time it takes to do each item
- not relying on a specific calendar daily
- not knowing how to prioritize.

These issues hold people back from successfully using To

Do lists. Yet, a working To Do list helps you to become more productive and to manage time better. Improved productivity and time management *feels* good, and leads to improvement in your outlook and attitude. Writing an effective list is the key. So let's look at how to overcome the underlying problems and make your To Do list your number-one tool for becoming organized.

Feeling as though To Do means should, must, or have to. Call it an Action List, or Today's Goals, or anything you like if To Do brings up negative connotations for you.

Trying to start your day by writing the list. Make tomorrow's list before you leave work today. As you come upon new tasks that you can't handle today, add them to tomorrow's list. Today's unfinished tasks can be carried over or eliminated. Throw out the old list and start fresh daily.

Believing it takes too long or wastes time to write the list. Look at it this way: it takes too long *not* to write the list. Taking a bit of time to plan ahead saves time in the long run. Lists help you stay focused, which increases your productivity. It's like a map, a track to run on. If you veer off, look at the list, and you're back on track.

Believing that lists or calendars don't work. It's not the list or calendar that doesn't work. It's your lack of knowledge or inconsistent use of it that isn't working.

Not knowing how to write it, what items to include. Write down anything you don't want to forget. Cross off items as you complete them to achieve a sense of satisfaction.

Including too many tasks. If more than 10 items are listed, some will probably not get done. Can't complete the entire list? No problem. Focus on completing the priorities and meeting due dates.

Confusing a daily list with a master list. A master list is comprised of all the things you'd like to do in the distant future. Add items from it to your daily list as time allows. Another issue is confusing projects with tasks. Projects usually consist of several steps. Break projects down into their steps, or tasks, then add these individual tasks to your daily list.

Not looking at the list often enough or losing it. Each day is a new adventure. In order not to lose your way, keep your road map (your list) handy. Locate it in the same place each day, such as the right corner of your desk. Also, use the same type of paper daily—for example, a 5" x 7" sheet of pastel- or neon-colored paper—to make your list easy to spot. And remember it is important not to pile other things on top of it!

Underestimating the time it takes to do each item. Running out of time is a major cause of frustration with To Do lists, contributing to their failure. Double the amount of time you think you'll need for each task. This will also help you prevent over-scheduling.

Not relying on a specific calendar daily. Pick one calendar and use it exclusively. Write all your business and personal appointments, due dates, and deadlines into your calendar as they arise. Then refer to your calendar daily when preparing tomorrow's To Do list.

Not knowing how to prioritize. Prioritize by time blocks. If you have five minutes available, choose something off the list that will take five minutes to do. If you have a two-hour block, look on the list for an appropriate activity to fill it. Also, consider your energy level. Do easy, short tasks when you're tired. Schedule intense tasks for peak energy times.

Remember, To Do lists are tools that help you navigate

through your day. So, in the immortal words of Toby Keith, "Start livin', that's the next thing on my list."

CHAPTER 16
10 SMART PACKING TIPS

We all travel, some of us more often than others. Those of us who travel all the time probably have packing down to a system. For the rest of us, though, being organized with our packing can be difficult because we don't do it on a regular basis. Following are 10 tips to make packing easier.

1. Make a list of every activity in which you will be participating. Pull out the clothes you'll need for each. Don't forget to include travel time. Will you be on a plane, train, bus, or automobile? Dress for comfort.

2. When traveling by plane, wear comfortable shoes for that long hike through the concourse and while carrying your baggage. Also, make sure your shoes are easy to take on and off when going through security checkpoints.

3. Color co-ordinate all your outfits. Black, blue, and brown are good basics. They can be spruced up by accessorizing with colorful ties or scarves.

4. Shoes take up a lot of space. Narrow them down to a few pairs that go with most outfits. Stuff shoes with underwear and socks, placing them on the bottom of your suitcase, along with heavier items.

5. Choose easy-care fabrics such as cotton, poly-blends, washable silks, and light knits. Bring packets of Woolite or Delicare to wash out underwear, socks, and stockings at night. They will be dry by morning.

6. Wrinkles can't be avoided completely, but they can be minimized. Pack clothes tightly so they don't move around. Packing suits, dresses, shirts, and blouses in plastic dry cleaning bags helps. Placing a sheet of tissue paper between each layer of folded clothing, then folding the clothes backwards also helps. You might want to pack spray products such as Wrinkle Free or Downy Wrinkle Releaser, which are suitable for most fabrics.

7. Roll your pajamas, nightgowns, t-shirts, belts, and other casual clothes to fit in small spaces.

8. Pack toiletries in leak-proof containers and resealable plastic bags. Place bottles of shampoo and conditioner in plastic-sealed bags, too, as they tend to leak.

9. Since luggage can be lost or delayed during air travel, pack a separate carry-on bag with a change of clothing and underwear, medications, essential toiletries, make-up, jewelry, your itinerary, passport, and tickets. A copy of prescriptions for medications and eyeglasses could also prove useful. Valuables should never be carried in checked baggage. Note: contact the airline regarding current security restrictions. There are limits as to how many fluid ounces you can bring aboard, as well as on various toiletries.

10. Place luggage tags on each suitcase or box being shipped. It may be safer for women to use only first initials on these tags. Additionally, include a paper with your home address and itinerary inside the bag.

Be sure that old airline baggage tags and bar code strips are removed from your luggage.

With these tips, your successful trip is assured. You won't be panicking at the last moment about lost or forgotten items. Store the Lifetime Travel List from the following chapter with your luggage or in a travel file for future use during packing.

CHAPTER 17
YOUR LIFETIME TRAVEL LIST

How many times have you left on a trip, only to discover you've forgotten something? Sometimes that something is inconsequential. Other times you feel like kicking yourself.

Packing can be stressful. Just when you think you're done and you've snuggled into bed, ready to leave in the morning, "one more thing" enters your mind. Or, you're ready to leave, but can't shake that tugging feeling that you've forgotten something. Making a list (and checking it twice) can smooth out the stress of packing.

I have compiled a master list to help you. Use the list as a guide and adjust it to your specific needs, depending upon the nature of your trip. For example, going on a business trip alone, driving the kids to Grandma's for a few days, flying to Bali for your honeymoon, or going fly fishing for the weekend each call for different packing criteria.

If you have children, you probably have other items to add to this list. If you have a baby, you will certainly have more items to add. Your circumstances will determine which additional items are needed to customize your list. Expect the list to evolve and change over the years as your circumstances change.

Copy this list, place it in a sheet protector, then keep it handy with other travel items. Refer to it every time you pack.

Before you start packing, refer to the list as a guide. After you think you're done packing, use it as a checklist. Scan it over several times during the packing process.

A Few Last Things to Do Before Leaving

- Adjust the temperature control to use less energy, or turn it off.
- Arrange for a house and pet sitter.
- Ask your neighbor to pick up your mail, or put it on hold.
- Change your voice mail message.
- Empty the garbage.
- Feed the pets.
- Forward your e-mail or put it on auto-response.
- Leave emergency contact numbers.
- Plug in the light timer.
- Reduce the temperature in your refrigerator.
- Reserve the airport shuttle.
- Set the alarm.
- Stop newspaper delivery.
- Synch or charge your electronics.
- Unplug the television, computer, and other electronics that won't be used.
- Water the plants.
- Write house and pet care instructions for the sitter.

I think you will find that these simple lists reduce your stress and start your trip on a happy note. There is no substitute for being organized.

Clothing
Belts
Blouses
Boots
Coats
Collar stays
Cuff links
Dresses
Girdles
Gloves
Gowns
Handkerchiefs
Hats
Jackets
Jeans
Jewelry
Pajamas
Panties
Raincoat
Robes
Scarves
Shirts
Shoes
Skirts
Slacks
Slippers
Slips
Socks
Stockings
Suits
Sweaters
Sweatshirts
Shorts
Ties
Tie pins

Incidentals
Address book
Air freshener
Airline ticket/E-ticket
Diary/journal
Diet sugar
Digital camera/charge
Dressy purse
Dust buster
Ear phone (headphones)
Ear plugs
Electronics
(IPOD/radio/DVD player)
Flashlight
Games
Gifts
Hangers
Instant hand sanitizer
Iron
Laptop computer/charger
Locks/keys
Luggage tags
Magazines/books
Maps/atlas
PDA (e.g. Palm Pilot)
Pens/pencils
Pillows
Plastic bag for dirty clothes
Playing cards
Purse
Scissors
Sewing kit
Small cooler
Smoke detector
Snacks and gum
Sporting goods equipment
Sunglasses
Sun/golf hat

Toiletries
After shave
Creams/lotions
Comb
Cotton balls
Dental floss
Deodorant
Depilatory
Electric shaver
Face soap
Facial tissues
Hair brush
Hair dryer/flat iron
Hair products
Hair rollers/clips
Hair spray
Hairpiece/wig
Magnifying mirror
Makeup
Manicure items
Mouthwash/floss
Perfume/cologne
Razor/blades
Shampoo/conditioner
Shaving cream
Shower cap
Soap/dish
Sun block
Tissues
Toothbrush/paste
Tweezers

Medical
Antihistamines
Band-aids
Calamine lotion
Cotton swabs
Diarrhea medicine
Eye cup/drops
Eyeglasses/contact lenses
Foot powder
Hot water bottle
Ice bag
Indigestion remedy
Insect repellent
Medicine spoon
Laxative
Motion sickness medication
Nasal spray
Lip balm
Pain reliever
Petroleum jelly
Prescription medicines
Rubbing alcohol
Sanitary needs
Skin cleanser
Sleeping pills
Tampons/pads
Thermometer

International
Electrical converter
Language dictionary
Passport
plus one copy

DIANE A. HATCHER-CPO®

CHAPTER 18
WHY HIRE A PROFESSIONAL ORGANIZER?

The National Association of Professional Organizers (NAPO) defines a professional organizer as "a person who provides ideas, information, structure, solutions and systems to increase productivity, reduce stress, save time and energy, and lead to more control over time, space and activities." This definition has been expanded to include that a professional organizer "enhances the lives of clients by designing systems and processes using organizing principles, and through transferring organizing skills. A professional organizer also educates the public on organizing solutions and the resulting benefits."

Services run the gamut from residential organizing—including kitchens, closets, home offices, and garages—to business organizing, which includes desks, offices, filing systems, and time management. Other services include wardrobe consulting, project management, records management, packing/unpacking and moving, space planning, computer consulting, insurance organizing, errands, and shopping. Some organizers specialize in Feng Shui, a facet of interior design that works with *chi* (energy flow) to enhance prosperity, harmony, and happiness. Other organizers specialize in redesign and staging.

Training

Although no formal course work is required, professional

organizers are trained through NAPO conference workshops, books, courses, seminars, tapes, sharing with other organizers, and their natural tendency toward being organized. Beginning in 2007, NAPO is implementing certification for experienced organizers that will provide a prestigious professional designation however will not be a requirement.

The National Study Group on Chronic Disorganization (NSGCD) is another group that provides education for professional organizers. Its primary interest is studying and researching physical, emotional, and mental issues that effect one's organizing ability. Example issues include AD/HD (Attention Deficit/Hyperactivity Disorder), OCD (Obsessive Compulsive Disorder), hoarding, traumatic brain injury, physical challenges, and chronic disorganization. (See Chapter 4.) Knowledge of the effects of these physical and psychological factors on disorganization helps professional organizers serve their clients more effectively.

Professional vs. Self-Help

Sometimes people say that their spouse, friend, or co-worker is very organized and can help them, so they don't need a professional. In some cases, this may be true. However, there are drawbacks. There is an old saying, "You don't know what you don't know." We've all heard about parents who try to teach their child to drive, or spouses who try to teach their partner how to play tennis, each with disastrous results. Being naturally organized doesn't mean one knows how to help someone who isn't. Criticism, misunderstandings, and judgment can be devastating to an already emotional, disorganized person.

Bookstores are stocked with organizing books that provide great ideas. However, as with most self-help books, results can be limited. Reports indicate that people tend to benefit more quickly and successfully when working with a professional who is customizing systems and solutions designed to meet their needs.

A good professional organizer is non-judgmental, encouraging, motivating, and patient. She helps you stay focused, and establishes simplified systems customized to meet your style and needs. By not imposing her own will on you, the emotional aspect that could lead to conflict is removed.

Scope

Jobs vary in scope. A housewife needs help dealing with the inevitable piles of mail that seem to magically multiply on the kitchen table. A salesman's filing system has no rhyme or reason to it, and he misses deadlines. A successful professional woman has areas of her home so full of clutter that she is overwhelmed and embarrassed. She feels frustrated and depressed at the sight. The partners in a firm are very organized but frustrated at the inefficiency of their staff. These are all actual situations remedied by professional organizers.

Fees

Fees vary by geographic location, type of job, and an organizer's experience. They can range from $50 to $200 per hour, with one- to four-hour minimums per session. Some organizers offer group seminars to businesses or to the public.

Time for Action

If you feel hesitant about contacting an organizer, ask yourself these questions to identify what is holding you back:

- Am I hesitant about someone seeing my private papers?
- Do I fear criticism?
- Am I embarrassed for anyone to see my mess?
- Am I thinking that I should be able to do this myself?
- How committed am I to getting organized?

These are typical issues that keep people from scheduling an organizing appointment. Remember, though, an organizer is not a guest in your house. She is a non-judgmental professional committed to confidentiality. Like I said in the first chapter, there's no need to be embarrassed to see a doctor when you are ill, right? There's no need to feel embarrassed in having an organizer see your clutter, either. That is what organizers see and do everyday. It's their job.

When choosing an organizer, ask questions. Are they members of NAPO? Do they have experience in the areas you need? Do they sound professional? Are they good listeners? Are your personalities compatible? Will they provide references?

Check out www.napo.net, www.onlineorganizing.com, www.organizerswebring.com, or Google to locate an organizer in your area.

There Is Hope

Do you think you are beyond help? Don't despair! Given the right kind of help, anyone can learn to be more organized.

Generally, disorganization can be attributed to one of several factors: mistakes in your organizing system, external situations, or internal forces. A professional organizer can identify the causes of your condition and help you implement an effective, lasting solution that you can easily maintain.

Getting organized is not a painful process. It's a matter of breaking some old habits and disciplining one's self to create new ones. Professional organizers can help guide you through the process. They will not only help you clean up and get caught up, they will teach, coach, and train you how to get organized, then set up systems individualized for your specific needs so that you can stay organized. There really is no better time than now to get organized!

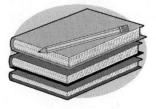

CHAPTER 19
SCHEDULING A DAY IN

Getting organized is such a high-interest topic that NAPO designated the entire month of January as National Get Organized Month. But there's no need to wait until January to get organized. Now is as good a time as any to start.

If your home or office is in need of major organizing, I suggest you schedule a day (or days) to work on it. Write it on your calendar as an appointment with yourself. After all, things don't organize themselves. Nor does knowing how to organize do any good unless you implement what you know. Here are some tips from the experts for getting started.

Set aside a specific time. This might be a weekend or evening if you can't afford time during the week. Stick to your planned schedule. If dedicating a full day to organizing isn't feasible, schedule blocks anywhere from 15 minutes to two hours long until the project is completed.

Set the mood. Put on your most comfortable clothes, then put on some lively music. You'll move faster and keep your spirits up.

Take care of your body. Eat a good breakfast in order to give yourself energy. Drink lots of water as you work.

Start small. Once you have completed a small area (say, the file drawer in your desk), you will feel energized, accomplished, and motivated. This will encourage you to move onto another area.

Sort. Here's where riding the RAFT surfaces. Refer back to Chapter 8 for details.

Be ruthless. As you're sorting, keep asking yourself: "How long has it been since I've used this item?" If it's been a while, ask yourself why. Can you identify a realistic use for it? What would be the worse thing to happen if you tossed it? When sorting papers, have a trashcan or large bag handy. Throw out any papers that have expired or for which duplicates are available. Remember that 80% of what is filed is never referenced again. Be brutal, and pat yourself on the back for each filled bag.

Put items in their proper place. Put like with like, and put things where you use them.

Stay focused. Work only in one area at a time. Don't leave one room to bring items to other rooms. Don't let phone calls interrupt you. Keep the computer off. Remember to skim instead of getting bogged down in the papers' content.

Enjoy yourself. Notice how soon you start feeling good about what you're doing. Some describe this as a sense of freedom, others as control. Whatever it feels like to you, it's going to feel good, which will motivate you to do more.

Reward yourself. During the day, reward yourself with brief breaks, a favorite cup of coffee, or a cold soft drink— whatever motivates you.

Inch by Inch

Of course, there's no need to wait until everything is so disorganized that you spend days getting caught up. If this is your first attempt at organizing your office, then a full day (or more) might be needed. But once the area is organized, you will not have to spend as many hours on that area again *as long as you put things away promptly.*

Remember your grandparents saying, "Inch by inch, things are a cinch?" If you consistently do a little, things are accomplished more easily than if you let them build up. Therefore, why not do your organizing as it comes up? Put things back from where you took them. Put them where you use them. Open mail daily, and file at least weekly. When you bring new things in, put them away that day. In fact, never purchase anything unless you can answer two questions: What am I going to use it for and where am I going to put it? (My clients hear these words resonate in their ears when shopping.)

Another old saying applies: "A stitch in time, saves nine." Ah Grandma, you did know what you were talking about.

CHAPTER 20
ODE TO AN ORGANIZER

I have been inspired by many of my clients, and thus this poem was born. A little bit of humor goes a long way when you're trying to get organized. I dedicate this poem to all of you who are making the effort to be organized and to assure you that the outcome will be worth your time.

New Year's Day had come and gone.
Surveying the clutter, she sighed
And decided to set a goal:
"It's time to get organized."

Papers were stuffed in cupboards,
More papers teetered high on her desk,
Papers spewed from inside drawers to floors;
Goodness, what a mess!

Once, her office was a joy
But the mail was now piled so high,
Bills were not getting paid on time;
Keeping up wasn't worth the try.

Then the woman read a story
About someone who could help her,
And she thought she'd gone to heaven
When she dialed the phone number.

When the organizing pro came in,
A wizard with a plan,
She worked her magic, room by room,
While our friend muttered "Shazam!"

Her office returned to order,
Amazed, she toured from room to room,
Feeling peaceful inside and energized,
Rejoicing at every turn.

Clutter gone, drawers with room,
The desktop now had workspace
Her life had returned to normal;
Hope gave way to a smoother pace.

The moral of this story?
No one has to live with clutter.
Nor must you face chaos alone,
Call a professional organizer!

ABOUT THE AUTHOR

Diane Alterman Hatcher-CPO®, is a professional organizer, founder and owner of Time-Savers Professional Organizing Services, Inc. Since 1998, she has been custom designing organizing systems and solutions for paperwork, time management, clutter and productivity issues for both residential and business clients who want to improve their qualities of life. She specializes in assisting clients with Chronic Disorganization and paperwork issues.

In 2007, Diane became an elite member of the inaugural group of Certified Professional Organizers earning the designation CPO®.

A monthly columnist for the *Sun-Sentinel's Weston Gazette* from 1999 to 2006, Diane has also been featured in local newspapers, magazines, television, and radio. She has appeared in *Women's Day* and *Balance* magazines and is quoted in several organizing books, including *Organizing Plain and Simple* by Donna Smallin.

Diane has been the honorary recipient of the Davie-Cooper City Chamber of Commerce's Small Business Person of the Year, and the American Business Women's Association Spirit of Excellence Business Leader of the Year. Appointed by the Mayor, she served on Cooper City's Charter Review Board, and volunteers for the Broward Sheriff's Office.

Diane graduated from the University of Florida with a degree in Journalism and Communications and a major in

Public Relations. She holds teaching certifications (inactive) in elementary and early childhood education from Nova Southeastern University and St. Leo's College. She previously worked for major corporations in the insurance industry.

Diane loves being a professional organizer. It provides her the opportunity to share her knowledge and love of teaching and being organized, while assisting others who desire to become more organized reach their goals. She is a member of the National Association of Professional Organizers (www.napo.net), NAPO's Golden Circle and the National Study Group on Chronic Disorganization (www.nsgcd.org).

Diane and her husband, Don—both Florida natives—have been happily married since 1977. They live in Cooper City, FL and have two beautiful daughters.

For further tips and information please visit her website at www.timesaversusa.com.

ORDERING INFORMATION

For additional copies of this book send an
email to info@timesaversusa.com,
place an order at www.timesaversusa.com,
or call 954-252-7511.
Books also available from www.amazon.com.

Made in the USA